This journal belongs to:

_____

MY WALKING LIFE

MY WALKING LIFE

Where I Went, What I Saw Along
the Way, and How I Felt

———————————

SPRUCE BOOKS

A Sasquatch Books Imprint

"All truly great thoughts are
conceived while walking."

—Friedrich Nietzsche, *Twilight of the Idols*

WHY KEEP A WALKING JOURNAL?

"Walking is a defining human activity. Walking can be
practical, moving the body from place to place;
ceremonial, such as religious and secular processions;
spiritual, a pilgrimage or hike through a wilderness;
social, a stroll with a friend in a park; or political,
positioning the body in and through a contested zone."

—Heather Sealy Lineberry

Walking is so much more than just putting one foot in front of the
other. As noted above by sustainability scholar and art curator
Heather Sealy Lineberry, walking reflects and contains much of what
makes us human. We walk for fun, for exercise, and to get from one
place to another. We walk to see the sights, to take our pets and
children outdoors, to connect with a friend and be sociable—or to
move alone through space and time. We walk in protest and for con-
solation. We walk with purpose or without. We walk just because.

Walking offers a wealth of benefits for both physical and mental health. Numerous studies demonstrate that walking supports overall fitness and heart health, prevents weight gain, reduces the risk of developing cancer, diabetes, and other chronic illnesses, enhances strength and endurance, lowers blood pressure and cholesterol, and even improves posture. As for mental health, walking has been shown to reduce depression and anxiety, alleviate fatigue, while boosting mood, memory, and creative thinking.

And, of course, taking a walk is one of life's greatest pleasures.

This book provides a unique opportunity to combine the benefits of walking with those of journaling. Why should you take the time to write about your walks?

Science has plenty to say about journaling, with many studies offering evidence that, like walking itself, keeping a journal is a positive wellness practice that improves our sense of well-being, sharpens our memories, reduces our feelings of anxiety, and can even help lift us out of depression. Journaling focuses our attention, supports our mindfulness practice, and helps us process our feelings. Journaling about walking ultimately enhances our experience of both!

Indeed, writing about walking extends the enjoyment of the outing, bringing focus and mindfulness to the act of walking, capturing the memories and special moments that occur during walks, and creating a meaningful record of our perambulations that we can keep, revisit, and share.

This journal provides space to chronicle your walks—not just when, where, and who with, but also why you walked and what you learned, saw, or gained along the way. You'll have the chance to jot down the insights and ideas that walking often inspires; describe those funny, strange, or profound moments that you witnessed; and take notes about what you enjoyed or disliked about a particular route, occasion, or experience. Some fun prompts to get you thinking about your walking life in ways large and small are also included. You can compile your favorite walking playlists, dream about the walks you might one day take in scenic or special locations around the world, or jot down the details of which shoes you prefer for a comfortable stroll or which provide the best support for a rigorous hike. Your dog's favorite route, the leafy spot where you can see the most interesting birds, or the secret path that leads to a waterfall—there is room in this journal to record all the wonders of your walking life.

"Above all, do not lose your desire to walk:
every day I walk myself into a state of well-being
and walk away from every illness."

— Søren Kierkegaard

date .... / .... / ....   weather ....

location ....

destination ....
....
....

did I walk alone or in company? (list companions, humans or otherwise)
....
....
....
....

the route I took ....
....

why I chose this route ....
....

OVERALL ENJOYMENT OF THIS WALK

(1)————————(2)————————(3)————————(4)————————(5)

stumble   smooth   sublime

EXERCISE FACTOR

(1)————————(2)————————(3)————————(4)————————(5)

meandering   steady pace   power walk

what I noticed around me as I was walking ....
....
....

did I see anything new, unusual, or particularly interesting on this walk? ....
....
....
....

what I thought or talked about while walking ....
....
....

realizations, ideas, insights, or memorable thoughts that came up during this walk
....
....
....

gratitude moment ....
....
....

not-so-great moment ....
....
....

would I walk this way again?   Y   N
why or why not? ....
....
....
....

date .... /........./.........   weather ....

location ....

destination ....
....
....

did I walk alone or in company? (list companions, humans or otherwise)

....
....
....
....

the route I took ....
....

why I chose this route ....
....

OVERALL ENJOYMENT OF THIS WALK

(1)————————(2)————————(3)————————(4)————————(5)

stumble   smooth   sublime

EXERCISE FACTOR

(1)————————(2)————————(3)————————(4)————————(5)

meandering   steady pace   power walk

what I noticed around me as I was walking ....

....

....

did I see anything new, unusual, or particularly interesting on this walk? ....

....

....

....

what I thought or talked about while walking ....

....

....

realizations, ideas, insights, or memorable thoughts that came up during this walk

....

....

....

gratitude moment ....

....

....

not-so-great moment ....

....

....

would I walk this way again?   Y   N

why or why not? ....

....

....

....

date .... / .... / ....   weather ....

location ....

destination ....
....
....

did I walk alone or in company? (list companions, humans or otherwise)

....
....
....
....

the route I took ....
....

why I chose this route ....
....

OVERALL ENJOYMENT OF THIS WALK

①————————②————————③————————④————————⑤

stumble   smooth   sublime

EXERCISE FACTOR

①————————②————————③————————④————————⑤

meandering   steady pace   power walk

what I noticed around me as I was walking ....

....

....

did I see anything new, unusual, or particularly interesting on this walk? ....

....

....

....

what I thought or talked about while walking ....

....

....

realizations, ideas, insights, or memorable thoughts that came up during this walk

....

....

....

gratitude moment ....

....

....

not-so-great moment ....

....

....

would I walk this way again?   Y   N

why or why not? ....

....

....

....

date .... / .... / ....   weather ....

location ....

destination ....
....
....

did I walk alone or in company? (list companions, humans or otherwise)

....
....
....
....

the route I took ....
....

why I chose this route ....
....

OVERALL ENJOYMENT OF THIS WALK

(1)——————(2)——————(3)——————(4)——————(5)

stumble   smooth   sublime

EXERCISE FACTOR

(1)——————(2)——————(3)——————(4)——————(5)

meandering   steady pace   power walk

what I noticed around me as I was walking ....

....

....

did I see anything new, unusual, or particularly interesting on this walk? ....

....

....

....

what I thought or talked about while walking ....

....

....

realizations, ideas, insights, or memorable thoughts that came up during this walk

....

....

....

gratitude moment ....

....

....

not-so-great moment ....

....

....

would I walk this way again?   Y   N

why or why not? ....

....

....

....

date .... / .... / ....   weather ....

location ....

destination ....
....
....

did I walk alone or in company? (list companions, humans or otherwise)

....
....
....
....

the route I took ....
....

why I chose this route ....
....

OVERALL ENJOYMENT OF THIS WALK

①——————②——————③——————④——————⑤

stumble   smooth   sublime

EXERCISE FACTOR

①——————②——————③——————④——————⑤

meandering   steady pace   power walk

what I noticed around me as I was walking ....
....
....

did I see anything new, unusual, or particularly interesting on this walk? ....
....
....
....

what I thought or talked about while walking ....
....
....

realizations, ideas, insights, or memorable thoughts that came up during this walk
....
....
....

gratitude moment ....
....
....

not-so-great moment ....
....
....

would I walk this way again?   Y   N
why or why not? ....
....
....
....

date ..../......../........ weather ....

location ....

destination ....
....
....

did I walk alone or in company? (list companions, humans or otherwise)
....
....
....
....

the route I took ....
....

why I chose this route ....
....

OVERALL ENJOYMENT OF THIS WALK

(1)————————(2)————————(3)————————(4)————————(5)

stumble   smooth   sublime

EXERCISE FACTOR

(1)————————(2)————————(3)————————(4)————————(5)

meandering   steady pace   power walk

what I noticed around me as I was walking ....

....

....

did I see anything new, unusual, or particularly interesting on this walk? ....

....

....

....

what I thought or talked about while walking ....

....

....

realizations, ideas, insights, or memorable thoughts that came up during this walk

....

....

....

gratitude moment ....

....

....

not-so-great moment ....

....

....

would I walk this way again?   Y   N

why or why not? ....

....

....

....

date .... / .... / ....   weather ....

location ....

destination ....
....
....

did I walk alone or in company? (list companions, humans or otherwise)

....
....
....
....

the route I took ....
....

why I chose this route ....
....

OVERALL ENJOYMENT OF THIS WALK

①————————②————————③————————④————————⑤

stumble   smooth   sublime

EXERCISE FACTOR

①————————②————————③————————④————————⑤

meandering   steady pace   power walk

what I noticed around me as I was walking ....

....

....

did I see anything new, unusual, or particularly interesting on this walk? ....

....

....

....

what I thought or talked about while walking ....

....

....

realizations, ideas, insights, or memorable thoughts that came up during this walk

....

....

....

gratitude moment ....

....

....

not-so-great moment ....

....

....

would I walk this way again?   Y   N
why or why not? ....

....

....

....

WALKING AND LISTENING

Do you amble along while getting lost in a podcast? March briskly to the news? Have a curated playlist of favorite songs to power you on your way? Make a list of what you like to listen to—or develop a playlist for a future stroll.

....
....
....
....
....
....
....
....
....
....
....
....
....
....
....
....
....
....
....
....
....
....
....
....
....
....
....
....
....

date .... / .... / ....   weather ....

location ....

destination ....
....
....

did I walk alone or in company? (list companions, humans or otherwise)

....
....
....
....

the route I took ....
....

why I chose this route ....
....

OVERALL ENJOYMENT OF THIS WALK

①——————②——————③——————④——————⑤

stumble   smooth   sublime

EXERCISE FACTOR

①——————②——————③——————④——————⑤

meandering   steady pace   power walk

what I noticed around me as I was walking ....

....

....

did I see anything new, unusual, or particularly interesting on this walk? ....

....

....

....

what I thought or talked about while walking ....

....

....

realizations, ideas, insights, or memorable thoughts that came up during this walk

....

....

....

gratitude moment ....

....

....

not-so-great moment ....

....

....

would I walk this way again?   Y   N
why or why not? ....

....

....

....

date .... /........./.........   weather ....

location ....

destination ....
....
....

did I walk alone or in company? (list companions, humans or otherwise)

....
....
....
....

the route I took ....
....

why I chose this route ....
....

OVERALL ENJOYMENT OF THIS WALK

①————————②————————③————————④————————⑤

stumble   smooth   sublime

EXERCISE FACTOR

①————————②————————③————————④————————⑤

meandering   steady pace   power walk

what I noticed around me as I was walking ....

....

....

did I see anything new, unusual, or particularly interesting on this walk? ....

....

....

....

what I thought or talked about while walking ....

....

....

realizations, ideas, insights, or memorable thoughts that came up during this walk

....

....

....

gratitude moment ....

....

....

not-so-great moment ....

....

....

would I walk this way again?   Y   N

why or why not? ....

....

....

....

date ...... / .... / ....   weather ....

location ....

destination ....
....
....

did I walk alone or in company? (list companions, humans or otherwise)

....
....
....
....

the route I took ....
....

why I chose this route ....
....

OVERALL ENJOYMENT OF THIS WALK

(1)————————(2)————————(3)————————(4)————————(5)

stumble   smooth   sublime

EXERCISE FACTOR

(1)————————(2)————————(3)————————(4)————————(5)

meandering   steady pace   power walk

what I noticed around me as I was walking ....
....
....

did I see anything new, unusual, or particularly interesting on this walk? ....
....
....
....

what I thought or talked about while walking ....
....
....

realizations, ideas, insights, or memorable thoughts that came up during this walk
....
....
....

gratitude moment ....
....
....

not-so-great moment ....
....
....

would I walk this way again?   Y   N
why or why not? ....
....
....
....

date .... / .... / ....   weather ....

location ....

destination ....
....
....

did I walk alone or in company? (list companions, humans or otherwise)

....
....
....
....

the route I took ....
....

why I chose this route ....
....

OVERALL ENJOYMENT OF THIS WALK

①————————②————————③————————④————————⑤

stumble   smooth   sublime

EXERCISE FACTOR

①————————②————————③————————④————————⑤

meandering   steady pace   power walk

what I noticed around me as I was walking ....

....

....

did I see anything new, unusual, or particularly interesting on this walk? ....

....

....

....

what I thought or talked about while walking ....

....

....

realizations, ideas, insights, or memorable thoughts that came up during this walk

....

....

....

gratitude moment ....

....

....

not-so-great moment ....

....

....

would I walk this way again?   Y   N

why or why not? ....

....

....

....

date .... / .... / ....   weather ....

location ....

destination ....
....
....

did I walk alone or in company? (list companions, humans or otherwise)

....
....
....
....

the route I took ....
....

why I chose this route ....
....

OVERALL ENJOYMENT OF THIS WALK

1 ——— 2 ——— 3 ——— 4 ——— 5

stumble   smooth   sublime

EXERCISE FACTOR

1 ——— 2 ——— 3 ——— 4 ——— 5

meandering   steady pace   power walk

what I noticed around me as I was walking ....

....

....

did I see anything new, unusual, or particularly interesting on this walk? ....

....

....

....

what I thought or talked about while walking ....

....

....

realizations, ideas, insights, or memorable thoughts that came up during this walk

....

....

....

gratitude moment ....

....

....

not-so-great moment ....

....

....

would I walk this way again?   Y   N

why or why not? ....

....

....

....

date .... / .... / ....   weather ....

location ....

destination ....
....
....

did I walk alone or in company? (list companions, humans or otherwise)

....
....
....
....

the route I took ....
....

why I chose this route ....
....

OVERALL ENJOYMENT OF THIS WALK

(1)————(2)————(3)————(4)————(5)

stumble   smooth   sublime

EXERCISE FACTOR

(1)————(2)————(3)————(4)————(5)

meandering   steady pace   power walk

what I noticed around me as I was walking ....

....

....

did I see anything new, unusual, or particularly interesting on this walk? ....

....

....

....

what I thought or talked about while walking ....

....

....

realizations, ideas, insights, or memorable thoughts that came up during this walk

....

....

....

gratitude moment ....

....

....

not-so-great moment ....

....

....

would I walk this way again?   Y   N

why or why not? ....

....

....

....

date .... / .... / ....   weather ....

location ....

destination ....
....
....

did I walk alone or in company? (list companions, humans or otherwise)

....
....
....
....

the route I took ....
....

why I chose this route ....
....

OVERALL ENJOYMENT OF THIS WALK

(1)————(2)————(3)————(4)————(5)

stumble   smooth   sublime

EXERCISE FACTOR

(1)————(2)————(3)————(4)————(5)

meandering   steady pace   power walk

what I noticed around me as I was walking ....

....

....

did I see anything new, unusual, or particularly interesting on this walk? ....

....

....

....

what I thought or talked about while walking ....

....

....

realizations, ideas, insights, or memorable thoughts that came up during this walk

....

....

....

gratitude moment ....

....

....

not-so-great moment ....

....

....

would I walk this way again?   Y   N
why or why not? ....

....

....

....

A WELL—TRODDEN PATH

There are rewards to be found in treading a familiar path, getting to know its nuances, observing what changes over time and what stays the same, revisiting a route again and again. Write about a place you've frequently walked and why it is special to you.

favorite path #1 ....
....

why I keep coming back: ....
....
....
....

favorite path #2 ....
....

why I keep coming back: ....
....
....
....

favorite path #3 ....
....

why I keep coming back: ....
....
....
....

favorite path #4 ....
....

why I keep coming back: ....
....
....
....

favorite path #5 ....
....

why I keep coming back: ....
....
....
....

" . . . in these strolls in Summer eve's twilight;

I view again the scenes I love so well

And watch the gentle coming of the night."

—Ed Blair, "An Evening's Stroll"

date .... / .... / ....   weather ....

location ....

destination ....
....
....

did I walk alone or in company? (list companions, humans or otherwise)

....
....
....
....

the route I took ....
....

why I chose this route ....
....

OVERALL ENJOYMENT OF THIS WALK

①————②————③————④————⑤

stumble   smooth   sublime

EXERCISE FACTOR

①————②————③————④————⑤

meandering   steady pace   power walk

what I noticed around me as I was walking ....

....

....

did I see anything new, unusual, or particularly interesting on this walk? ....

....

....

....

what I thought or talked about while walking ....

....

....

realizations, ideas, insights, or memorable thoughts that came up during this walk

....

....

....

gratitude moment ....

....

....

not-so-great moment ....

....

....

would I walk this way again?   Y   N

why or why not? ....

....

....

....

date .... / .... / ....   weather ....

location ....

destination ....
....
....

did I walk alone or in company? (list companions, humans or otherwise)

....
....
....
....

the route I took ....
....

why I chose this route ....
....

OVERALL ENJOYMENT OF THIS WALK

①————————②————————③————————④————————⑤

stumble   smooth   sublime

EXERCISE FACTOR

①————————②————————③————————④————————⑤

meandering   steady pace   power walk

what I noticed around me as I was walking ....

....

....

did I see anything new, unusual, or particularly interesting on this walk? ....

....

....

....

what I thought or talked about while walking ....

....

....

realizations, ideas, insights, or memorable thoughts that came up during this walk

....

....

....

gratitude moment ....

....

....

not-so-great moment ....

....

....

would I walk this way again?   Y   N

why or why not? ....

....

....

....

date .... / .... / ....   weather ....

location ....

destination ....
....
....

did I walk alone or in company? (list companions, humans or otherwise)

....
....
....
....

the route I took ....
....

why I chose this route ....
....

OVERALL ENJOYMENT OF THIS WALK

(1)————————(2)————————(3)————————(4)————————(5)

stumble   smooth   sublime

EXERCISE FACTOR

(1)————————(2)————————(3)————————(4)————————(5)

meandering   steady pace   power walk

what I noticed around me as I was walking ....

....

....

did I see anything new, unusual, or particularly interesting on this walk? ....

....

....

....

what I thought or talked about while walking ....

....

....

realizations, ideas, insights, or memorable thoughts that came up during this walk

....

....

....

gratitude moment ....

....

....

not-so-great moment ....

....

....

would I walk this way again?   Y   N

why or why not? ....

....

....

....

WALKING THE WORLD

This world is full of spectacular walking routes: Spain's Camino de Santiago, the Pennine Way in the United Kingdom, Peru's Inca Trail, the Kumano Kodo in Japan, Canada's West Coast Trail, the Appalachian Trail in the United States. What faraway trails do you dream of tackling?

trail ....

....

location ....

....

why I'd like to walk it ....

....

....

....

trail ....

....

location ....

....

why I'd like to walk it ....

....

....

....

trail ....
....

location ....
....

why I'd like to walk it ....
....
....
....

trail ....
....

location ....
....

why I'd like to walk it ....
....
....
....

date .... / .... / ....   weather ....

location ....

destination ....
....
....

did I walk alone or in company? (list companions, humans or otherwise)

....
....
....
....

the route I took ....
....

why I chose this route ....
....

OVERALL ENJOYMENT OF THIS WALK

①————————②————————③————————④————————⑤

stumble   smooth   sublime

EXERCISE FACTOR

①————————②————————③————————④————————⑤

meandering   steady pace   power walk

what I noticed around me as I was walking ....

....

....

did I see anything new, unusual, or particularly interesting on this walk? ....

....

....

....

what I thought or talked about while walking ....

....

....

realizations, ideas, insights, or memorable thoughts that came up during this walk

....

....

....

gratitude moment ....

....

....

not-so-great moment ....

....

....

would I walk this way again?   Y   N
why or why not? ....

....

....

....

date .... / .... / ....   weather ....

location ....

destination ....
....
....

did I walk alone or in company? (list companions, humans or otherwise)

....
....
....
....

the route I took ....
....

why I chose this route ....
....

OVERALL ENJOYMENT OF THIS WALK

(1)————————(2)————————(3)————————(4)————————(5)

stumble   smooth   sublime

EXERCISE FACTOR

(1)————————(2)————————(3)————————(4)————————(5)

meandering   steady pace   power walk

what I noticed around me as I was walking ....
....
....

did I see anything new, unusual, or particularly interesting on this walk? ....
....
....
....

what I thought or talked about while walking ....
....
....

realizations, ideas, insights, or memorable thoughts that came up during this walk
....
....
....

gratitude moment ....
....
....

not-so-great moment ....
....
....

would I walk this way again?   Y   N
why or why not? ....
....
....
....

date .... / ..../ ....   weather ....

location ....

destination ....
....
....

did I walk alone or in company? (list companions, humans or otherwise)

....
....
....
....

the route I took ....
....

why I chose this route ....
....

OVERALL ENJOYMENT OF THIS WALK

①————————②————————③————————④————————⑤

stumble   smooth   sublime

EXERCISE FACTOR

①————————②————————③————————④————————⑤

meandering   steady pace   power walk

what I noticed around me as I was walking ....

....

....

did I see anything new, unusual, or particularly interesting on this walk? ....

....

....

....

what I thought or talked about while walking ....

....

....

realizations, ideas, insights, or memorable thoughts that came up during this walk

....

....

....

gratitude moment ....

....

....

not-so-great moment ....

....

....

would I walk this way again?   Y   N

why or why not? ....

....

....

....

date .... / .... / ....   weather ....

location ....

destination ....
....
....

did I walk alone or in company? (list companions, humans or otherwise)

....
....
....
....

the route I took ....
....

why I chose this route ....
....

OVERALL ENJOYMENT OF THIS WALK

(1)————————(2)————————(3)————————(4)————————(5)

stumble   smooth   sublime

EXERCISE FACTOR

(1)————————(2)————————(3)————————(4)————————(5)

meandering   steady pace   power walk

what I noticed around me as I was walking ....

....

....

did I see anything new, unusual, or particularly interesting on this walk? ....

....

....

....

what I thought or talked about while walking ....

....

....

realizations, ideas, insights, or memorable thoughts that came up during this walk

....

....

....

gratitude moment ....

....

....

not-so-great moment ....

....

....

would I walk this way again?   Y   N

why or why not? ....

....

....

....

"Walking takes longer . . . than any other known form of locomotion except crawling. Thus it stretches time and prolongs life. Life is already too short to waste on speed."

—Edward Abbey

MADE FOR WALKIN'

The right footwear is essential for an enjoyable walk. Jot down what you look for in a walking shoe or hiking boot as well as your preferred brands. Refer back to these notes when it's time to replace your kicks.

....
....
....
....
....
....
....
....
....
....
....
....
....
....
....
....
....
....
....
....
....
....
....
....
....
....
....
....
....
....
....
....
....

date ...... / .... / ....   weather ....

location ....

destination ....
....
....

did I walk alone or in company? (list companions, humans or otherwise)

....
....
....
....

the route I took ....
....

why I chose this route ....
....

OVERALL ENJOYMENT OF THIS WALK

(1)————————(2)————————(3)————————(4)————————(5)

stumble   smooth   sublime

EXERCISE FACTOR

(1)————————(2)————————(3)————————(4)————————(5)

meandering   steady pace   power walk

what I noticed around me as I was walking ....

....

....

did I see anything new, unusual, or particularly interesting on this walk? ....

....

....

....

what I thought or talked about while walking ....

....

....

realizations, ideas, insights, or memorable thoughts that came up during this walk

....

....

....

gratitude moment ....

....

....

not-so-great moment ....

....

....

would I walk this way again?   Y   N

why or why not? ....

....

....

....

date ……. / ……. / ……   weather ……………………………………………………………………………

location ………

destination ……
………
………

did I walk alone or in company? (list companions, humans or otherwise)

………………………………………………………………   ………………………………………………………………
………………………………………………………………   ………………………………………………………………
………………………………………………………………   ………………………………………………………………
………………………………………………………………   ………………………………………………………………

the route I took ……
………

why I chose this route …………………………………………………………………………………………………
………

OVERALL ENJOYMENT OF THIS WALK

(1)————————(2)————————(3)————————(4)————————(5)

stumble   smooth   sublime

EXERCISE FACTOR

(1)————————(2)————————(3)————————(4)————————(5)

meandering   steady pace   power walk

what I noticed around me as I was walking ....

....

....

did I see anything new, unusual, or particularly interesting on this walk? ....

....

....

....

what I thought or talked about while walking ....

....

....

realizations, ideas, insights, or memorable thoughts that came up during this walk

....

....

....

gratitude moment ....

....

....

not-so-great moment ....

....

....

would I walk this way again?   Y   N

why or why not? ....

....

....

....

date .... / .... / ....   weather ....

location ....

destination ....
....
....

did I walk alone or in company? (list companions, humans or otherwise)

....
....
....
....

the route I took ....
....

why I chose this route ....
....

OVERALL ENJOYMENT OF THIS WALK

①————————②————————③————————④————————⑤

stumble   smooth   sublime

EXERCISE FACTOR

①————————②————————③————————④————————⑤

meandering   steady pace   power walk

what I noticed around me as I was walking ....

....

....

did I see anything new, unusual, or particularly interesting on this walk? ....

....

....

....

what I thought or talked about while walking ....

....

....

realizations, ideas, insights, or memorable thoughts that came up during this walk

....

....

....

gratitude moment ....

....

....

not-so-great moment ....

....

....

would I walk this way again?   Y   N

why or why not? ....

....

....

....

date ..../......../........   weather ....

location ....

destination ....
....
....

did I walk alone or in company? (list companions, humans or otherwise)

....
....
....
....

the route I took ....
....

why I chose this route ....
....

OVERALL ENJOYMENT OF THIS WALK

①————————②————————③————————④————————⑤

stumble   smooth   sublime

EXERCISE FACTOR

①————————②————————③————————④————————⑤

meandering   steady pace   power walk

what I noticed around me as I was walking ....
....
....

did I see anything new, unusual, or particularly interesting on this walk? ....
....
....
....

what I thought or talked about while walking ....
....
....

realizations, ideas, insights, or memorable thoughts that came up during this walk
....
....
....

gratitude moment ....
....
....

not-so-great moment ....
....
....

would I walk this way again?   Y   N
why or why not? ....
....
....
....

date .... / .... / ....   weather ....

location ....

destination ....
....
....

did I walk alone or in company? (list companions, humans or otherwise)

....
....
....
....

the route I took ....
....

why I chose this route ....
....

OVERALL ENJOYMENT OF THIS WALK

①————————②————————③————————④————————⑤

stumble   smooth   sublime

EXERCISE FACTOR

①————————②————————③————————④————————⑤

meandering   steady pace   power walk

what I noticed around me as I was walking ....
....
....

did I see anything new, unusual, or particularly interesting on this walk? ....
....
....
....

what I thought or talked about while walking ....
....
....

realizations, ideas, insights, or memorable thoughts that came up during this walk
....
....
....

gratitude moment ....
....
....

not-so-great moment ....
....
....

would I walk this way again?   Y   N
why or why not? ....
....
....
....

THE ROADS TAKEN

What unforgettable strolls live on in your memory? Write down the walks you'll always remember.

when ....

where ....

with whom ....

why I remember it ....
....
....
....
....
....

when ....

where ....

with whom ....

why I remember it ....
....
....
....
....
....

when ....

where ....

with whom ....

why I remember it ....
....
....
....
....
....

when ....

where ....

with whom ....

why I remember it ....
....
....
....
....
....

date .... / ..../ .... weather ....

location ....

destination ....
....
....

did I walk alone or in company? (list companions, humans or otherwise)

....
....
....
....

the route I took ....
....

why I chose this route ....
....

OVERALL ENJOYMENT OF THIS WALK

①———————②———————③———————④———————⑤

stumble   smooth   sublime

EXERCISE FACTOR

①———————②———————③———————④———————⑤

meandering   steady pace   power walk

what I noticed around me as I was walking ....

....

....

did I see anything new, unusual, or particularly interesting on this walk? ....

....

....

....

what I thought or talked about while walking ....

....

....

realizations, ideas, insights, or memorable thoughts that came up during this walk

....

....

....

gratitude moment ....

....

....

not-so-great moment ....

....

....

would I walk this way again?   Y   N

why or why not? ....

....

....

....

date .... / .... / ....   weather ....

location ....

destination ....
....
....

did I walk alone or in company? (list companions, humans or otherwise)

....
....
....
....

the route I took ....
....

why I chose this route ....
....

OVERALL ENJOYMENT OF THIS WALK

①————————②————————③————————④————————⑤

stumble   smooth   sublime

EXERCISE FACTOR

①————————②————————③————————④————————⑤

meandering   steady pace   power walk

what I noticed around me as I was walking ....

....

....

did I see anything new, unusual, or particularly interesting on this walk? ....

....

....

....

what I thought or talked about while walking ....

....

....

realizations, ideas, insights, or memorable thoughts that came up during this walk

....

....

....

gratitude moment ....

....

....

not-so-great moment ....

....

....

would I walk this way again?   Y   N

why or why not? ....

....

....

....

date .... / .... / ....   weather ....

location ....

destination ....
....
....

did I walk alone or in company? (list companions, humans or otherwise)

....
....
....
....

the route I took ....
....

why I chose this route ....
....

OVERALL ENJOYMENT OF THIS WALK

(1)————————(2)————————(3)————————(4)————————(5)

stumble   smooth   sublime

EXERCISE FACTOR

(1)————————(2)————————(3)————————(4)————————(5)

meandering   steady pace   power walk

what I noticed around me as I was walking ....
....
....

did I see anything new, unusual, or particularly interesting on this walk? ....
....
....
....

what I thought or talked about while walking ....
....
....

realizations, ideas, insights, or memorable thoughts that came up during this walk
....
....
....

gratitude moment ....
....
....

not-so-great moment ....
....
....

would I walk this way again?   Y   N
why or why not? ....
....
....
....

"Happy is the person who has
acquired the love of walking
for its own sake!"

—W.J. Holland

GOOD COMPANY

Who do you like to walk with? Make a list of your favorite
companions from past or current walks—or come up with a
dream walking-buddy list.

date ...... / .... / ....   weather ....

location ....

destination ....
....
....

did I walk alone or in company? (list companions, humans or otherwise)

....
....
....
....

the route I took ....
....

why I chose this route ....
....

OVERALL ENJOYMENT OF THIS WALK

(1)——————(2)——————(3)——————(4)——————(5)

stumble   smooth   sublime

EXERCISE FACTOR

(1)——————(2)——————(3)——————(4)——————(5)

meandering   steady pace   power walk

what I noticed around me as I was walking ....

....

....

did I see anything new, unusual, or particularly interesting on this walk? ....

....

....

....

what I thought or talked about while walking ....

....

....

realizations, ideas, insights, or memorable thoughts that came up during this walk

....

....

....

gratitude moment ....

....

....

not-so-great moment ....

....

....

would I walk this way again?   Y   N
why or why not? ....

....

....

....

date ...... /........./........   weather ....

location ....

destination ....
....
....

did I walk alone or in company? (list companions, humans or otherwise)

....
....
....
....

the route I took ....
....

why I chose this route ....
....

OVERALL ENJOYMENT OF THIS WALK

(1)———————(2)———————(3)———————(4)———————(5)

stumble   smooth   sublime

EXERCISE FACTOR

(1)———————(2)———————(3)———————(4)———————(5)

meandering   steady pace   power walk

what I noticed around me as I was walking ....

....

....

did I see anything new, unusual, or particularly interesting on this walk? ....

....

....

....

what I thought or talked about while walking ....

....

....

realizations, ideas, insights, or memorable thoughts that came up during this walk

....

....

....

gratitude moment ....

....

....

not-so-great moment ....

....

....

would I walk this way again?   Y   N

why or why not? ....

....

....

....

date .... / .... / ....   weather ....

location ....

destination ....
....
....

did I walk alone or in company? (list companions, humans or otherwise)

....
....
....
....

the route I took ....
....

why I chose this route ....
....

OVERALL ENJOYMENT OF THIS WALK

(1)————————(2)————————(3)————————(4)————————(5)

stumble   smooth   sublime

EXERCISE FACTOR

(1)————————(2)————————(3)————————(4)————————(5)

meandering   steady pace   power walk

what I noticed around me as I was walking ....

....

....

did I see anything new, unusual, or particularly interesting on this walk? ....

....

....

....

what I thought or talked about while walking ....

....

....

realizations, ideas, insights, or memorable thoughts that came up during this walk

....

....

....

gratitude moment ....

....

....

not-so-great moment ....

....

....

would I walk this way again?   Y   N

why or why not? ....

....

....

....

date .... / .... / ....   weather ....

location ....

destination ....
....
....

did I walk alone or in company? (list companions, humans or otherwise)

....
....
....
....

the route I took ....
....

why I chose this route ....
....

OVERALL ENJOYMENT OF THIS WALK

①————————②————————③————————④————————⑤

stumble   smooth   sublime

EXERCISE FACTOR

①————————②————————③————————④————————⑤

meandering   steady pace   power walk

what I noticed around me as I was walking ....

....

....

did I see anything new, unusual, or particularly interesting on this walk? ....

....

....

....

what I thought or talked about while walking ....

....

....

realizations, ideas, insights, or memorable thoughts that came up during this walk

....

....

....

gratitude moment ....

....

....

not-so-great moment ....

....

....

would I walk this way again?   Y   N
why or why not? ....

....

....

....

MAP MY ROUTE

Make a map of a walking route that you think you know well, labeling the main places or sights. What are the landmarks? The street names? Is there anyone you see regularly along the way? A frequent stopping point? Even if you don't consider yourself someone who can draw, try to make a sketch (and don't judge it—just have fun).

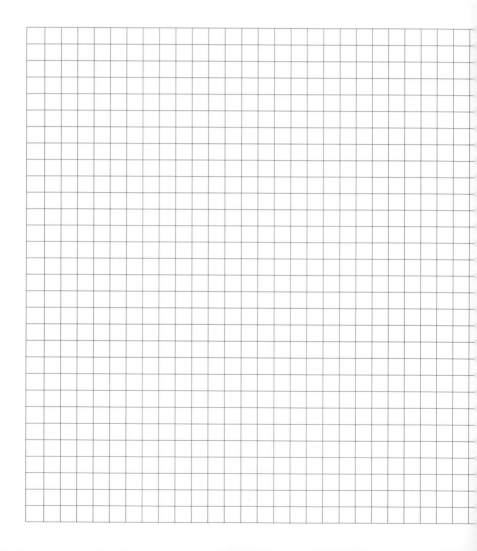

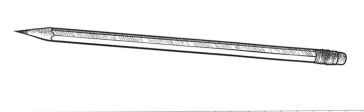

date .... / .... / ....   weather ....

location ....

destination ....
....
....

did I walk alone or in company? (list companions, humans or otherwise)

....
....
....
....

the route I took ....
....

why I chose this route ....
....

OVERALL ENJOYMENT OF THIS WALK

(1)———————(2)———————(3)———————(4)———————(5)

stumble   smooth   sublime

EXERCISE FACTOR

(1)———————(2)———————(3)———————(4)———————(5)

meandering   steady pace   power walk

what I noticed around me as I was walking ....

....

....

did I see anything new, unusual, or particularly interesting on this walk? ....

....

....

....

what I thought or talked about while walking ....

....

....

realizations, ideas, insights, or memorable thoughts that came up during this walk

....

....

....

gratitude moment ....

....

....

not-so-great moment ....

....

....

would I walk this way again?   Y   N

why or why not? ....

....

....

....

date .... / .... / ....   weather ....

location ....

destination ....
....
....

did I walk alone or in company? (list companions, humans or otherwise)

....
....
....
....

the route I took ....
....

why I chose this route ....
....

OVERALL ENJOYMENT OF THIS WALK

(1)———————(2)———————(3)———————(4)———————(5)

stumble   smooth   sublime

EXERCISE FACTOR

(1)———————(2)———————(3)———————(4)———————(5)

meandering   steady pace   power walk

what I noticed around me as I was walking ....

....

....

did I see anything new, unusual, or particularly interesting on this walk? ....

....

....

....

what I thought or talked about while walking ....

....

....

realizations, ideas, insights, or memorable thoughts that came up during this walk

....

....

....

gratitude moment ....

....

....

not-so-great moment ....

....

....

would I walk this way again?   Y   N

why or why not? ....

....

....

....

date .... / .... / ....   weather ....

location ....

destination ....
....
....

did I walk alone or in company? (list companions, humans or otherwise)

....
....
....
....

the route I took ....
....

why I chose this route ....
....

OVERALL ENJOYMENT OF THIS WALK

(1)————————(2)————————(3)————————(4)————————(5)

stumble   smooth   sublime

EXERCISE FACTOR

(1)————————(2)————————(3)————————(4)————————(5)

meandering   steady pace   power walk